Call & Response

Produced By
Dr. Evelyn Bethune
Contributing Writers
Hobson Bethune, Sr.
Hobson Bethune, II
Marcia Bethune
Rashad Bethune
Robert Bethune
Sara Bethune
Elizabeth Bethune
Charles Miller, Jr.

Copyright © 2015
Bethune Publishing – The Bethune Group
Dr. Evelyn Bethune
First Printing

All rights reserved, including the right to reproduce this work in any form whatsoever without written permission from the publisher, except for brief passages in connection with a review. Photographs may not be reproduced without permission of the owner.

For information write:
Bethune Publishing House, Inc.
P. O. Box 2008
Daytona Beach, FL 32115-2008
docbethune@tbginc.org

Jacket designed by
John-Mark McLeod
J2maginations, LLC
J2maginations@gmail.com

Book design and page layout by
Bethune Publishing House, Inc.
Printed in the United States of America
Library of Congress Control Number: 2016900981
ISBN 978-0-9971548-0-1

TABLE OF CONTENTS

INTRODUCTION	1
LOVE	3
HOPE	7
CHALLENGE	13
THIRST	21
POWER	28
FAITH	33
DIGNITY	39
DESIRE	45
RESPONSIBILITY	49
ELIZABETH	57
PERSIST & ENDURE	62
A Poem for Mickel	69
JARVIS	72

Introduction

My desire to know God better is ongoing but over the years I have learned that I never have to feel alone or unworthy. Jesus paid it all and by His stripes I am truly healed. I took a different approach once I started to be obedient to the direction that God has for me. I am able to stand up in some of the most difficult times and rejoice in the knowledge that I am first forgiven and most importantly, loved by a God who knows no limitations. My story is one of triumph over adversity and it is not a unique story. There are thousands if not millions of stories just like mine. What makes it different is that it is mine. I have used it to heal others and to open doorways to dialog that allow me to guide others. I am a motivational speaker as well as an author but I am also a believer with a testimony of how God can bring you through the fire as pure gold, if you will simply let Him.

Call & Response is a continuation of the Legacy of Dr. Mary McLeod Bethune. Her words in The Last Will and Testament were a charge to keep, filled with strength for the journey ahead. Now generations later, we respond to those words in order to encourage others. Grandchildren great grands, and so forth, we are family. We have grown up in the shadow and the light of Mother Dear's greatness and in doing so we have learned that we too have a responsibility to meet the challenge. Our response cannot ever be in words alone but in our thoughts, words and deeds.

    Mary McLeod Bethune loved to sing This Little Light of Mine and she let her light shine, shine, shine, so that others could find their way. We must take on that same responsibility if our children and their children are to reach higher heights. We have all we need to stabilize our communities, but we must have a mindset that is unafraid, willing to share and determined to complete the task ahead.

The Legacy Continues…

LOVE

I LEAVE YOU LOVE: **(MMB)** Love builds. It is positive and helpful. It is more beneficial than hate. Injuries quickly forgotten quickly pass away. Personally, and racially, our enemies must be forgiven. Our aim must be to create a world of fellowship and justice where no man's skin, color or religion, is held against him. "Love thy neighbor" is a precept which could transform the world if it were universally practiced. It connotes brotherhood, and, to me, brotherhood of man is the noblest concept in all human relations. Loving your neighbor means being interracial, inter-religious and international.

I LEAVE YOU LOVE (Evelyn): The
greatest gift that you can give is what God gives to us…unconditional love. Love surpasses all boundaries. The differences of Race, religion, class, color, creed, political views, and even educational level, "quickly pass away" when we lead with love. Unconditional love allows for mistakes and forgiveness for ourselves as well as for others. You see, when we are able to open our hearts through love, it is, as a dear friend once told me, like flushing your brain. All that old stuff just goes down the drain and you are transformed. Love is not just for others but it is a healer for the giver. Mary McLeod Bethune believed in the absolute power of love to overcome the obstacles placed before her. She achieved because she loved.

I LEAVE YOU LOVE: (Hobson, SR)
Love is a foundation for positive relationships. God asks us to love each other as we love him. This love we should have for each other is the foundation on which we build trust and understanding, vital ingredients in our quest to work together in building businesses and communities that serve our people's best interest. There are far too many of our young that may know of God's love but don't feel it coming from each other. My Grandmother's

wish was not for us just to love each other, but to let that love be felt. "To know love and not share that love, is worst than not knowing at all". When we first love our fellowman and women, all good things are possible.

I LEAVE YOU LOVE: (SARA) The most wonderful thing you can do in this world is to love someone. To understand what God meant by "Love thy neighbor"; to transcend over color or religious beliefs is the link for which God wants all of us to strive.

HOPE

I LEAVE YOU HOPE. **(MMB)** The Negro's growth will be great in the years to come. Yesterday, our ancestors endured the degradation of slavery; yet they retained their dignity. Today, we direct our economic and political strength toward winning a more abundant and secure life. Tomorrow, a new Negro, unhindered by race taboos and shackles, will benefit from more than 330 years of ceaseless striving and struggle. Theirs will be a better world. This I believe with all my heart.

I LEAVE YOU HOPE (Evelyn):

Without hope, there is no movement. Without hope no future growth can be accomplished. Without hope, faith cannot exist. Hope is the legacy that guides us and allows us to draw our strength from it. It is Hope that opens our minds to dream bigger dreams and press forward in Faith, knowing that the possibilities are real. Our grandmother built institutions in the Hope that those she left behind would do good things, even greater than what she accomplished. Her HOPE for us was a vision of world peace and the determination to develop communities that would be self determining. The systematic erosion of HOPE for the future, erosion of Hope for a better day than the one our ancestors encountered, erosion of Hope for stability is placing us in the position of having to re-learn trust in each other and trust in something greater than our human selves. We have come too far to turn around now, and we must anchor our hope in bigger dreams that call us to action.

For without action, the Hopes of past generations will be lost and the future will hold even greater struggles. Today it is necessary to use our Faith as the lamp in darkness and make Hope for a better day our action plan as we make this world better inspite of the movement to push us backwards.

I LEAVE YOU HOPE. (Hobson Sr.)

Far too many of our people HOPE that their Dad or Mother or Uncle or Aunt would stop the drug abuse that has made them unproductive and unavailable to love and care for them and provide guidance by setting a proper example. Far too many of our people HOPE that someone in their life will change from a life of crime, where over two million of our people are incarcerated and so many more checked out of living productive lives due to drug abuse. My grandmother's HOPE for a solution to the injustices of prejudices was our involvement in this country's economic and political growth. That HOPE has to be reignited in all African Americans with a clear understanding that we all have a stake in the future of this country and our people. A HOPE rooted with dignity and respect for self and family. My Hope is that every child will live by the creed, "I won't do anything that might embarrass my parents", and every parent walking the path of "I won't do anything that might embarrass my children". The Hope of our people to prosper begins with the strength of our FAMILY.

I LEAVE YOU HOPE (Robert).

We live in a time where it is far too popular to do the wrong thing than it is to do right. My people do not value their lives and the lives of their brothers and sisters due to a lack of knowledge of our greatness. My HOPE is for my people to regain that greatness through knowledge of our ancestors' glory, before the degradation of slavery and wake up from this mental slavery that we are trapped in.

I LEAVE YOU HOPE (Sara): Hope to believe that the color of your skin should never be the reason for not having all of the things God desires for you. Hope means that you do not get stuck in the past but look to the future, to where you are going in the years ahead. We must all hope to be the leaders to a better world by directing others to economic growth and greater political awareness. Hope means that you never give up.

I LEAVE YOU HOPE (CJ)

Hope is something that is needed to survive in today's time and era. Without hope there wouldn't be any motivation or reason to chase your dreams. It's good to have hope so when times are hard you have some sort of inspiration to fall back on and to boost you back up. Everyone has a bad day or even a bad stretch of days but having hope tends to get you back to where you once were.

CHALLENGE

I LEAVE YOU THE CHALLENGE OF DEVELOPING CONFIDENCE IN ONE ANOTHER. (MMB)

As long as Negroes are hemmed into racial blocks of prejudice and pressure, it will be necessary for them to band together for economic betterment. Negro banks, insurance companies and other businesses are examples of successful racial economic enterprises. These institutions were made possible by vision and mutual aid. Confidence was vital in getting them started and keeping them going. Negroes have got to demonstrate still more confidence in each other in business. This kind of confidence will aid the economic rise of the race by bringing together the pennies and dollars of our people and plowing them into useful channels. Economic separatism cannot be tolerated in this enlightened age, and it is not practicable. We must spread out as far and as fast as we can, but we must also help each other as we go.

I LEAVE YOU THE CHALLENGE OF DEVELOPING CONFIDENCE IN ONE ANOTHER. (Hobson, Jr.) The confidence we should have in each other has been crippled during certain periods for centuries by a philosophy started by the infamous slave trader "Willie Lynch". The practice of tying each limb of a black man to a different horse and ripping his body apart in front of his woman and his child, forcing that mother to protect her male child by teaching him to be submissive to the slave owner to prevent a similar fate. That same philosophy instructed slave owners in the south to aggressively and consistently use our physical differences against us. Dark skinned against light skinned, educated against the uneducated, and the list goes on. With over a million Black men incarcerated and the majority of our black households headed by mothers we now have a generation of black youth led by a hip-hop culture fed by a system owned by white men. White men that control many parts of the music industry that are only interested in making as much money as they can through the labor of black artist, with no regard for the effect on the black community.

Its hard for a black boy growing up to have confidence in other black men when the one he should have had as an example is locked up and absent. His role models now are gangster rappers that wear their pants like prison inmates and treat women like whores. The reaction to this is our youth are raising themselves, with the boys wanting to be gangsters and our girls dressing the role they've been handed as sex symbols. There are so many obstacles today that hinder our cooperation with each other that it becomes evident that we have to take this challenge as serious as death itself. We must work together, putting our collective resources and energy on the same path toward maintaining the integrity of our people. My grandmother wrote in the 1950's what it takes today for our race to be morally and financially sustained. We must understand that there is a war against our people, an unconventional war that will end our existence if we don't have confidence in each other and work together. It doesn't mean that we won't work with other peoples or that we don't love other peoples, just that we must first love each other and work with each other, for the betterment of our people.

*I LEAVE YOU THE CHALLENGE OF DEVELOPING CONFIDENCE IN ONE ANOTHER (*Hobson Sr.*):*

Since the practice of doctrine introduced by the infamous "Willie Lynch", we've been on the back of the bus as far as working together as a people. The media portrays a picture of harmony amongst our people that have achieved success, but this has to be a grass roots process where the common laborer can work with his brother starting a business and having mutual trust in attaining sustained success. We've stood by and watched ethnic groups from all over the world come to America in search of the "American Dream" and realize it to more of an extent than we. Black people helped build this country and before any other races of people "make it" here, we must get on board and challenge the "status quote". We repeat the words too often that black people can't work together, letting sinful things like greed, jealousy, and egos destroy working relationships before they get off the ground or make any long term difference. We must put all our energies into developing Black Businesses and support them faithfully, even when it means traveling a little further to that Black owned business or spending a little more because that black business owner can't purchase their goods for the same price as his bigger competition. Those of us in business have to understand also the basic principles of business by establishing a faithful customer base by ensuring those customers are treated with the utmost respect. To the point that regardless of the cost, they shop with you because they are treated properly.

Too many times we here the stories of observing our own people treating whites better when served than we treat each other. They may have more money than us but they are not better than us. They may dress nicer than us but they are not as sincere. And as soon as they have to make the choice of supporting either black or white, that line was drawn in the sand many years ago. It's still there. We must start by being worthy of the trust of our fellow blacks, making us worthy of the trust of any people. We do this by starting with, "I can control my attitude and my actions, they will be positive. That control will influence the attitude and actions of those around me, making them positive. My little piece of the world can indeed influence the world, a little bit at a time, but eventually, the entire world." (Hobson Bethune, 2007)

I LEAVE YOU THE CHALLENGE OF DEVELOPING CONFIDENCE IN ONE ANOTHER (Sara):

A Challenge is always a good thing. It is God's way of pushing us to do better. We must over come the "crabs in the bucket" way of thinking and the "*I got mine*" mentality. We should never forget about each other and help each other by sharing information and leading the way. We do this not only by working hard but by getting a good education and then teaching someone else. "Each one, teach one" and then let's see how far we can go.

I LEAVE YOU THE CHALLENGE OF DEVELOPING CONFIDENCE IN ONE ANOTHER (Robert):

In order for Black people in America to gain the respect and status that is well overdue, we will have to learn to believe in each other. In today's time, it seems that our people have negative things to say about one another. If a young black male in this country drives a nice car or wears nice clothes, he did something illegal to gain those mentioned possessions. This is a warped view of African Americans in this country. Yes, this may indeed go on, but let's not focus on the negative. There are plenty of educated and successful entrepreneurs in this country. Our goal as a people should be to nourish the theme of hard work and dedication, rather than behaviors that are self destructive to our people as a whole.

I LEAVE YOU THE CHALLENGE OF DEVELOPING CONFIDENCE IN ONE ANOTHER (CJ)

Trust your brothers and sisters. Don't try to take on life alone. In a world where you are different you need support and encouragement from your neighbor. Trust your neighbor to do the rights things for the community.

THIRST

***I LEAVE YOU A THIRST FOR EDUCATION.* (MMB)** Knowledge is the prime need of the hour. More and more, Negroes are taking full advantage of hard-won opportunities for learning, and the educational level of the Negro population is at its highest point in history. We are making greater use of the privileges inherent in living in a democracy. If we continue in this trend, we will be able to rear increasing numbers of strong purposeful men and women, equipped with vision, mental clarity, health and education.

Now that the barriers are crumbling everywhere, the Negro in America must be ever vigilant lest his forces be marshaled behind wrong causes and undemocratic movements. He must not lend his support to any group that seeks to subvert democracy. That is why we must select leaders who are wise and courageous, and of great moral stature and ability. We have great leaders among us today. We have had other great men and women in the past; Frederick Douglas, Booker T. Washington, Harriet Tubman, Sojourner Truth, and Mary Church Terrell. We must produce more qualified people like them, who will work not for themselves, but for others.

I LEAVE YOU A THIRST FOR EDUCATION (Hobson): Over one hundred years have passed since my grandmother opened the doors to her school for black children, beginning the opening of so many doors of educational institutes to our people. We can't let the sacrifices of those that made these paths through hatred and bigotry be forgotten. Dr. Mary McLeod Bethune, had a vision; and as she believed, we must, that through honest effort and the fact that God exists in all people, we have the strength to fight the fight against injustice. And so true today as she envisioned a century ago, education is the greatest weapon against the dependency on a systematically unjust society.

The struggle of her generation seemed insurmountable, followed by monumental advances achieved by the generation behind her, led by men of integrity like Dr. Martin Luther King Jr. and the Honorable Malcolm X. The torch of faith that fueled the hope of those individuals has been torn away from the hands of the masses of our people, not only with the bullets that ended the lives of those much needed leaders before their time, but also with seeds of hate planted in our people against each other through doctrine of the likes of slave trader and owner Willie Lynch.

Seeds of hate are like weeds in a garden.

Without a gardener that truly loves the garden, those weeds mingle themselves deep amongst the roots of the flowers. Similar to those weeds, the hatred of our people passed down through generations, is just as hungry, perpetuating inadequate public schools and an unjust criminal justice system. The struggle continues as we are at war. A war that takes our kids through a public education system that targets them for dependence on self pity and low-esteem. The spirit of African American boys is suppressed to the point that by grades 6 and 7, their thirst for new knowledge has turned into a hate of school where they can't be themselves. Being taught primarily by white women that don't understand them and don't have enough love for them to tap in on their energy and keep their thirst for knowledge and new experiences alive. It is now having a profoundly negative effect on our girls as well.

    Our schools today look so much like they did 30 years ago. The integration fought for so vigorously in the 60's has transitioned into a new form of segregation. Inner city school now house just as large a percentage of minorities as before the civil rights marches of the 60's and 70's. Over recent years there has been an alarming decrease in the number of black males attending college creating a disproportionate gap between black males and black females attending college. The number one contributor to this alarming fact is that thousands of college age black males are either in prison or killing each other on the streets. Our need as a people for independence, enhanced tremendously through education, can not be left up to the streets to be accomplished. We must support the schools that educate, encourage our kids to attend those schools, and demand their excellence. Our continued education as a people will end the slavery, forever.

I LEAVE YOU A THIRST FOR EDUCATION. (**Evelyn**) Today it seems that the thirst for education has been quenched with an illusion. An illusion that we are treated and will be treated equal while this country continues to falter its efforts towards equality. We as African Americans must look toward the past for the resolve our ancestors had. They believed in themselves for the answers to their problems. Today this country builds prisons instead of schools. The penal system has become the place where most of our youth end up, especially our young males. Some may argue against the theory of conspiracy towards our males, but it's hard to accept the fact that although we make up only 13 percent of the countries population, we make up more than 50 percent of the prison

population. With the advent of prisons industries, the past is thrust upon us. Slaves helped build this county even though it was wrong and evil, and today prison industries (legalized slavery) continues to rob our race of its bright talent. We must never cease the fight to stop the drugs and crime that allows our young to be caged in prisons instead of being taught the wonders of the world in schools.

I LEAVE YOU A THIRST FOR EDUCATION. (Robert)

To gain knowledge is a wonderful thing and my people need to strive to better themselves through education. Attending college and getting a good job is not all my people need. Knowledge of self is what's lacking amongst blacks to only become educated in the achievements of others will only continue to weaken the black race. My black brothers and sister need to become more educated about who they really are and where they came from so that we can stop being puppets aspiring to someone else's American Dream.

I LEAVE YOU A THIRST FOR EDUCATION: (Sara)

Even today, in 2012, the need for access to a good education is almost overpowering. Our children have been lost in the X Generation of video games and "gangsta" rap, making idols of "one hit wonders". Most of them have lost the understanding of a good education and the possibilities that it brings. Knowing how to manage your own money and understanding your place in a global economy can take your life to a different level but without an education and knowledge of self, you become seriously limited.

I LEAVE YOU A THIRST FOR EDUCATION (CJ)

Don't settle for a mediocre mind. Absorb as much information as possible. In this day and time the more you know the better off you would be.

POWER

I LEAVE YOU RESPECT FOR THE USES OF POWER. (MMB) We live in a world which respects power above all things. Power, intelligently directed, can lead to more freedom. Unwisely directed, it can be a dreadful, destructive force. During my lifetime I have seen the power of the Negro grow enormously. It has always been my first concern that this power should be placed on the side of human justice. Now that the barriers are crumbling everywhere, the Negro in America must be ever vigilant lest his forces be marshalled behind wrong causes and undemocratic movements. He must not lend his support to any group that seeks to subvert democracy.

That is why we must select leaders who are wise, courageous, and of great moral stature and ability. We have great leaders among us today: Ralph Bunche, Channing Tobias, Mordecai Johnson, Walter White, and Mary Church Terrell. [The latter now deceased]. We have had other great men and women in the past: [Frederick Douglass](), [Booker T. Washington](), [Harriet Tubman](), and [Sojourner Truth](). We must produce more qualified people like them, who will work not for themselves, but for others.

I LEAVE YOU RESPECT FOR THE USES OF POWER. (Hobson) This is such a major topic in relationship to the world we live in today. Even more so than it was half a century ago because of the advances in technology that makes our world so much smaller. Words spoken or actions taken on one side of the world are heard and seen all over the world in a matter of seconds. The so-called leaders of our people today were in many cases products of that technology. Since the end of the civil rights era we have been cast as followers of self proclaimed leaders that are in some cases just as corrupt morally as individuals that have taken action against our people. We live today in a country that claims to support democracy throughout the world, yet demonstrates a gross disregard for life, liberty, and freedom for people of color, most notably within the confines of the United States itself. The treatment of immigrants of color that wish for a better life in America are sent back, while lighter skinned immigrants are granted asylum if they only reach this country's shores. We only have to look at Haitian immigrants versus the treatment of Cuban and Mexican immigrants. We live in a country that's governed by big business. That power machine has dictated not only the actions of this country in regard to other countries, but in a very disappointing way in how the so-called leaders of our people have conducted themselves. Be it religious or political leadership, we have lacked in morally sound, "do as I do" leadership since the end of the civil rights movement of the 1950's and 1960's. In order to properly respect power we must know what power really is. The difference between real power and perceived power is the action behind the power. What is done with the power? We all have certain powers. The power within our choices. God gives us the free will to make choices for ourselves, whether they good or bad. This is the power we must respect. Our power of free will to act according to God's word. And lastly, look closely toward those that want to lead and study not only their words, but their deeds as well. There are many today that have a perceived power that has been perpetuated through their showmanship and charisma. There's a big difference between someone that is compelled by a "calling", to teach me through example the right path to chose and one that chooses to tell me what path I must take because it's a profitable business. That means to me that in the absence of sound leadership, I will not just follow anyone that wants to be a leader. We must have fellowship amongst ourselves, be responsible and hold each other accountable.

God made man in an image or himself, therefore he dwells within man. Not just a few selected men, but in all men. What happens next is the acknowledgement of that presence and then the actions that reflect

I LEAVE YOU A RESPECT FOR POWER: (Sara) To have true power, one must respect the manner in which it was received. The world leaders of today are lost in their own thinking. They make decisions in a vacuum and are foolish with the lives of millions with only the words from their own minds to guide them. Those in power must take care to listen to the wisdom of others. They must learn to respect power and maintain a true balance between the two.

FAITH

I LEAVE YOU FAITH. (MMB)

Faith is the first factor in life devoted to service. Without faith nothing is possible. With it, nothing is impossible. Faith in God is the greatest power, but great, too, is faith in oneself. In years, the faith of the American Negro in himself has grown immensely, and is still increasing. The measure of our progress as a race in precise relation to the depth of the faith in our people is held by our leaders. Frederick Douglass, genius though he was, was spurred by a deep conviction that his people would heed his counsel and follow him to freedom. . Our greatest Negro figures have been imbued with faith. Their perseverance paid rich dividends. We must never forget their suffering and their sacrifices, for they were the foundations of the progress of our people.

I LEAVE YOU FAITH. (Hobson Sr.)

The foundation laid by our forefathers through their sacrifice, hard work, and persecution was possible chiefly through their faith. Beginning, not so much a faith in mankind, but with a faith in themselves to take whatever skills they possessed, putting it on the line with the faith that Almighty God would direct. On this day and those to follow we must first believe in ourselves, for God dwells within, and act on that faith for the betterment of our people. The progress made by African Americans in this country would truly amaze my grandmother, yet disappointed she'd be in the state of our people as a whole. W.E.B. Dubose spoke many years ago of a talented tenth among our people that would take care of the rest. He felt that this would be accomplished through their leadership and direction. We have in this country many success stories among our people, yet there is still far too many of our people left behind and not a part of this great American Dream. I believe that many of us that have succeeded in our business and religious endeavors have failed our people. This is not to judge anyone on their short comings but to open for thought in each of us, our contributions to our people. If you're able to feed yourself with resources left over, have you feed anyone unable to provide for them self? If you've been successful in business, have you mentored or helped another succeed? If you profess to be saved, have you attempted to lead someone else toward their salvation? These are questions we can honestly answer through the kind of faith my grandmother had. Strength through faith can make us all better people. I have a personal story involving faith that I'd like to share with you. Many years ago I attended the Million Man March in Washington DC and was amazed at the fellowship I experienced while there. I only regretted not bringing my sons to witness the brotherhood shared by the Black men from all over the country. My faith was strong enough for me to make the long drive from Georgia to Washington but not strong enough to take my sons into the possibility of danger. What is really amazing about that story is the fact that it took an act of terrorism to make the entire country feel the way that most African Americans have felt since slavery. We've been the victim of acts of terrorism through out history to the point that we have always traveled cautiously. I've been a different person since that experience, in that my faith is stronger.

I LEAVE YOU FAITH: (Hobson, Jr.) Faith in others to do the right thing is

paramount in us developing strength and confidence in each other. Staying positive and believing that we all want the best for ourselves and each other is one of the most powerful tools we can use. The saying, "If you can't say anything positive, don't say anything at all," is very true in our dealings with each other. As race of people we must always be encouraging to each other and nurture our strength and faith in God.

I LEAVE YOU FAITH: (Robert)

Faith in God is very important in the development of Black people. Faith in each other is also important in our growth. This force will give us the momentum to push forward for racial equality. In our pursuit, we should not look toward anyone but ourselves. We should set our own standards and provide our own stamp of approval of what is acceptable.

I LEAVE YOU FAITH: (Sara)

One who lives without faith shall be lost in his own madness. Faith gives us the strength to see things no one else can and gives us peace of mind in the midst of hard times.

I LEAVE YOU FAITH (CJ)

Having faith during your darkest times is essential to spiritual and mental survival.

Having faith doesn't assure you will come out on top but it does keep you spiritually and mentally ready when "God's plan" finally kicks in. Faith can't be bought but it comes from within yourself. Believing that good will come your way eventually is faith.

DIGNITY

I LEAVE YOU RACIAL DIGNITY. I want Negroes to maintain their human dignity at all costs. We, as Negroes, must recognize that we are the custodians as well as the heirs of a great civilization. We have given something to the world as a race and for this we are proud and fully conscious of our place in the total picture of mankind's development. We must also learn to share and mix with all men. We must make an effort to be less race conscious and more conscious of individual and human values. I have never been sensitive about my color has never destroyed my self respect nor has it ever caused me to conduct myself in such a manner as to merit the disrespect of any person. I have not let my color handicap me. Despite many crushing burdens and handicaps, I have risen from the cotton fields of South Carolina to found a College, administer it during the years of growth, become a public servant in the government and country and a leader of women. I would not exchange my color for all the wealth in the world, for had I been born white, I might not have been able to do all I have done or yet hope to do.

I LEAVE YOU RACIAL DIGNITY

(Hobson, Sr.) Our dignity as a people has eroded into a self-fulfilling ideology practiced by too many. "Do you like me? What can you do for me? How we are viewed by others is merely a reflection of how we see ourselves. When we abuse our bodies with drugs and treat each other with little or no respect, how can we expect other peoples to view us differently? Our younger generation has adapted a dress code that includes sagging pants, dreaded hair, and ornamented teeth, which in most translations, associates the wearer with a "gangster" persona. Prisoners are not allowed to have belts, so most inmates have sagging pants. Another observation is that those with very sagging pants are available sexually for other inmates. With such a disproportionately large percentage of black males either in or just released from prison, that this way of wearing their pants transmits a terrible message to our youth. Do we want our youth emulating prisoners? Is this in some way paying tribute to those lost in the criminal justice system?

There is currently a big debate as to the use of the "N" word. One side of the debate understands the negative connotations associated with the word "nigger" and stress the importance of refraining from its use. The argument is based primarily on the premise that other races of people feel that if we use it to refer to each other, then why can't they use it also. That notion feeds that idea that the use of the word nigger when referring to black people contributes to negative stereotyping, and acts of bigotry, both passive and active.

I LEAVE YOU RACIAL DIGNITY:

(Robert) Racial dignity will be key in improving our self outlook. How we view ourselves is in direct correlation with how we will make positive strides to a collective success. Without dignity, you have nothing. If you don't respect yourself, you cannot possibly expect others to respect you. With a strong faith in GOD and self, nothing is impossible. We must learn to focus on the important things that need to be done and put forth the necessary actions to accomplish them. Therefore, racial dignity is instrumental in the elevation of the African American people.

I LEAVE YOU RACIAL DIGNITY:

(Evelyn) My grandmother never let her color stand in the way of her will to achieve what she wanted. She realized the greatness of the human spirit in overcoming adversity we face everyday. Her faith and belief in GOD propelled her heights even she didn't dream possible. Her resolve for racial equality allowed her to see thru the color line and look at the heart of a man. She believed that there is good in all of us and we must continue to trust that GOD will help us someday get to the point of racial dignity, shared, expressed, and given by all of us, to all of us.

I LEAVE YOU RACIAL DIGNITY:

(Sara) *Self*-respect in one's race is a power like no other. As leaders of this world, Black people must show human dignity at all times. We cannot allow others to determine who we are or force us to feel less than because of our race. We have proven that we are a people of great dignity because we have endured great challenges but achieved much in spite of attempts to disrespect us. We have pursued excellence even when doors were closed to us because of our race and we will continue to grow stronger as we learn, from the lightest to the darkest, to love ourselves even more.

I LEAVE YOU RACIAL DIGNITY (CJ)

Everyone is different. It's no one's fault what they look like but people are responsible for how they treat other people. Be kind because you never know who you may be conversing with and what trials they may be going through. As a black person you must keep your composure even when times are hard.

DESIRE

I LEAVE YOU A DESIRE TO LIVE HARMONIOUSLY WITH YOUR FELLOW MEN: (MMB)

The problem of color is worldwide. It is found in Africa and Asia, Europe and South America. I appeal to American Negroes -- North, South, East and West -- to recognize their common problems and unite to solve them.

I pray that we will learn to live harmoniously with the white race. So often, our difficulties have made us hypersensitive and truculent. I want to see my people conduct themselves naturally in all relationships -- fully conscious of their manly responsibilities and deeply aware of their heritage. I want them to learn to understand whites and influence them for good, for it is advisable and sensible for us to do so. We are a minority of 15 million living side by side with a white majority. We must learn to deal with these people positively and on an individual basis.

I LEAVE YOU THE DESIRE TO LIVE HARMONIOUSLY WITH YOUR FELLOW MEN. (Hobson Sr.)

Long before I read of or really knew of my grandmother's contributions to her people and mankind in general, I learned from my mother Mrs. Elizabeth S. Bethune and my father Mr. Albert McLeod Bethune, Sr., that we should treat people the way we wanted to be treated. My parents taught me that when one suffers, we all suffer. We still to this day live in a country where color matters. That being the case, we must work even harder to bridge gaps between ourselves and society. We must treat all people the way we want to be treated. Where there is mutual respect between African Americans and people of other races the possibility exists for mutual trust and accomplishment. It all starts within each of us, then spreads within our people, then spreads into the hearts and minds of those that may learned incorrectly that we are like animals.

I LEAVE YOU THE DESIRE TO LIVE HARMONIOUSLY WITH YOUR FELLOW MAN: (Sara)

Our grandmother knew that peace would require that we learn to live harmoniously with our fellow man even when they choose other wise.

For Black people it is still difficult to live in peace with whites. People all over the world still have problems living together and only by changing our thinking will we be able to co-exist in harmony. We must be more excepting of differences and more willing to resolve conflict through collaboration and consensus. The youth of today have a greater opportunity to change the world as they have greater exposure to people of different races, religions, ethnicities, etc. where one is not seen as the master of the other. This allows for open dialogue and the possibilities of getting to know each other without the obstacles of the past being insurmountable. It is important however that we also remember the importance of sustaining our culture and heritage and not feel that we must give up who we are in order to fit into the mainstream.

I LEAVE YOU THE DESIRE TO LIVE HARMONIOUSLY WITH YOUR FELLOW MAN (CJ)

Peace in the community. There is strength in numbers so make peace with your neighbor not enemies. As a black it is expected to be barbaric with your neighbor. Much can get done when the community can take on a challenge together.

RESPONSIBILITY

I LEAVE YOU FINALLY, A RESPONSIBILITY TO OUR YOUNG PEOPLE. (MMB)

The world around us really belongs to youth, for youth will take over its future management. Our children must never lose their zeal for building a better world. They must not be discouraged from aspiring toward greatness, for they are to be the leaders of tomorrow. Nor must they forget that there are masses of our people still underprivileged, ill-housed, impoverished and victimized by discrimination. We have a powerful potential in our youth, and we must have the courage to change old ideas and practices so that we may direct their power toward good ends.

I LEAVE YOU FINALLY, A RESPONSIBILITY TO OUR YOUNG PEOPLE (Hobson)

Our responsibility to the youth of our community is perhaps our greatest task. For no matter what accomplishments realized today, they amount to nothing if the youth of today cannot continue that success. We know that the youth of today are our future leaders and in this ever-evolving technological world we live in, our youth not only have to overcome domestic obstacles, they must also be able to compete internationally. We have a public-school system that has failed our youth terribly. Suppressing their energies and spirit for the sake of conformity to standards designed indifferent to their needs.

The questions addressing these failures highlight a lack of concern or love for our kids in the schools they must attend, very little parental participation, and standardized test that replace fundamental curriculums that produced scholars in the past. All these fronts have to be addressed and one of the most effective is having a responsible adult active in the development of each of our youth.

This is accomplished by taping into the community for mentors to work one-on-one with our youth as boosters for those that don't have the parental support necessary for their success. There are coaches that work with our youth in sports that need to understand their impact on the overall development of our youth and be trained to maximize their influence. Area colleges are also full of potential mentors that should receive college credit for long term participation in mentoring programs. This one aspect of mentoring not only enhances the chances of the youth's success; it also introduces college students to the idea of their enormous impact on the community through their service. Any adult with role model characteristics should be a mentor for a youth, either in the community or within their extended family.

The responsibility to our youth extends far beyond the guidance of teachers and parents. That burden should be shouldered by all of us. If we don't know how to help we should learn. When we know, we must teach. When we teach one, we reach one.

I LEAVE YOU FINALLY, A RESPONSIBILITY TO OUR YOUNG PEOPLE: (Robert)

The youth in this country have it more difficult than ever. With all that's available to them, it is easy to become distracted from one's priorities. It's up to the parents to develop a foundation on the difference between right and wrong. Yet many parents are missing in action too. Now a day it seems the subject of right and wrong is a bit cloudy in the minds of black youth. With music videos, movies, and video games so accessible to kids, it is almost impossible to keep their attention for longer than five minutes. We need to start early in the children's lives, teaching the importance of school, patience, and dedication to completing a task.

Today's public-school system will need to raise the bar in academic achievement, expecting excellence not making it the exception to the rule. Too many of our youth are leaving school with little or no education to stand on. Once they are placed in competition with their "non-black" counterparts, they believe there is really no contest because they have been made to feel inferior all their lives. We need to overcome this stigmatism and *shine* like God intended. It is important that our youth are equipped with the necessary tools and know how to survive in today's society. It is our job to make it happen. Our daddy used to say that his job was not done until we were successful. We still have work to do and not a lot of time to get it done.

I LEAVE YOU FINALLY A RESPONSIBILITY TO OUR YOUNG PEOPLE. (Evelyn) That's perhaps the greatest legacy that was left by my Grandmother. The young shall inherit the earth and it is all of our responsibility to equip them with everything they need to prepare them for the challenges they'll face. Our purpose in life is to make this place better than it was before. If we all assume that responsibility, reach one, teach one, help one, love one. When you help one you help us all.

Today we must be reminded that our young people are the fruit of our labor. They are the product of what we sewed. To paraphrase Psalms 100:3, *"It is we that have made them and not them themselves"*. If there is anything missing from their lives it is because "we" did not provide it.

All too often we speak of our youth as "bad", ill prepared for the future, lacking in skills and full of themselves. We say they are selfish, the "me" generation and we fear both them and our future with them.

Who do we think produced this product? It was not someone else. It was us. We planted the seed and sat back and let them rear themselves. We became friends, not parents. We didn't pull the weeds when needed, we let the weeds win. It was more important that our children like us than respect us and now we don't like the end result. Now we have a product, in many cases that we don't recognize, and we have given their care over to someone else, ANYBODY ELSE. Too often that "ANYBODY ELSE" is the prison system.

The challenge left to us my Dr. Mary McLeod Bethune is to be responsible for our young people. It is critical that we give them examples that they can understand, teach them to care about their fellow man and their communities and be anchored in their faith. We must ensure that they are equipped for the journey ahead and then get out of their way and let them grow.

I LEAVE YOU FINALLY A RESPONSIBILITY TO OUR YOUNG PEOPLE: (Sara)

As a parent, the greatest responsibility we have is to our children I say that as the mother of three young men of excellence. It is the responsibility of parents to get our young people to understand the power they have and the potential they bring as guardians of the future. They must be given the tools to stay away from harm and to over come discrimination. We must equip them to not be victims or allow fear to cause them to get stuck and lose their dreams. They must be given hope for the future so that they look ahead with dreams of making the future better. Our responsibility to them is to ensure that they know they matter and that how they live their life is as important as what they want to be in life.

I LEAVE YOU FINALLY, A RESPONSIBILITY TO OUR YOUNG PEOPLE (CJ)

Responsibility is key to maturing. Be accountable for your actions and accepting the good with the bad for your actions. Be responsible for your community. If there is a problem in the community stand up and take action instead of talking about it. If you're not helping the situation you are part of the problem and your responsibility is to be aware of your actions. This makes you a better person for your family and community.

Young people are the future. We can't let the young people fall behind and get off track. Encourage them to be better than they've ever thought they could be. Young people need to know the potential they have and how important they are to everyone else's future.

ELIZABETH
A Great Grand-Daughter

I am sitting at the gravesite of my great grandmother, known to the world as Dr Mary McLeod Bethune, but to our family as *Mother Dear*. Looking around at my fellow students as they prepare for graduation honors, I am continually amazed how a woman, a black woman, the descendant of former slaves and the first one of her 16 siblings born free, created this opportunity for me and others. She willed this opportunity out of her spirit, out of her undying thirst for knowledge and justice. In graduating from Bethune-Cookman

College I realize, finally, that the journey is just beginning.

I may never know what took me so long to appreciate and value her sacrifices, but I am grateful that I finally felt her spirit in me. How dare I come from such greatness and choose to live in mediocrity, to live a life of self-servitude? The mere thought that I can choose to be educated is a blessing all in itself. I have come to understand that being average means being the best of the worse and the worse of the best. My great grandmother set the tone for greatness and I have her genes in me. I had to understand what that meant before I was open enough to meet the challenge. Today, I am open to the possibilities.

After ten years of procrastination and avoidance, I finally heard her in my thoughts and spirit. I heard her speak to me; I saw the gifts she laid before me. I listened, and I took action. I had to come to my senses to accept my gift and not be afraid of my cross to bear that comes with service to others. I completed my Criminal Justice Degree during the 100-year anniversary of Bethune-Cookman College as a member of the first class to receive their degree from a woman president, since Dr. Bethune retired as the head of Bethune-Cookman College in 1947. Dr. Trudie Kibbie Reed stated that this was a historical, moment for the college but it is also a defining moment in my life. I had completed what I started, and I knew that *Mother Dear* would be proud. But I also knew the race was just beginning and I was still thirsty.

In the Last Will and Testament of Dr. Mary McLeod Bethune, she states that she leaves us a "thirst for knowledge". Approaching my graduation date left me feeling parched because *my thirst* grew stronger, the thirst she always talked about... *Mother Dear* placed within us the thirst for knowledge. She was right when she stated, in the 1930s, that *"knowledge is forever and will always be the key to freedom"*. My desire is now stronger, and a new thirst parches my mind and will only be quenched by a consumption of knowledge. I know that I have to reach for the high ground and prepare for the challenges ahead for there is a great need in my community for sincere leadership, mentors for the next generation and role models who are not afraid to shine light in the dark places. That was the example left to me by my great grandmother and the need today is as strong as it was 100 years ago, if not greater.

What now, I ask myself? What can I give back to the community, as she did? What can I do that will make a positive difference in society today as she has made a century before me? What shapes the meaning of our very existence? "The Law", I said, and suddenly, it all became clear. Just as Dr. Mary McLeod Bethune fought to change the laws that oppressed our people and change the opinions of others during her time, so have I seen the need to continue that work, continue her legacy, her worthwhile dream, for as she said:

> *"Faith is the first factor in a life devoted to service. Without it, nothing is possible. With it, nothing is impossible."*

She believed that if every person would just do their part to make the world a place of peace and equality for everyone, we would achieve our dreams. Her dream is now my dream. Just as an Olympic torchbearer passes the torch until eventually it lights the eternal flame, I too carry a light, a fire ignited from the eternal flame of knowledge, perseverance, achievement and service. I want to do my part.

Obtaining a law degree will allow me to ensure that her dream, my dream, our dreams are kept alive by giving hope and sometimes fighting for change, *YES*, sometimes changing the very laws of the land were made to hold us back. I want to be a part of creating, maintaining and defending, the laws that allow us to feel protected and promote self-sufficiency while helping is to become contributing members of society.

My wish is the wish of my great grandmother, that I continue to grow and strive for excellence in everything that I do. Not for my sole benefit but for the betterment of those that come behind me. Let me clear a path so others may have a safer journey. I eagerly "Enter to learn, depart to serve" as I go forward as Dr. Mary McLeod Bethune did, "not for myself but for others."
Mary McLeod Bethune (1875 - 1955) Educator/Activist/Dreamer

Great Granddaughter
Elizabeth Bethune

Persist & Endure

Love is the greatest gift that we can give to the world and to those with whom we come in contact. Everything else grows out of that beginning. With it, the harvest is bountiful and continues to produce for generations. Without it your fields lie fallow and the fruit is bitter.

As a family we are a product of greatness. We did not choose our ancestry, God did and because of that, we can never turn our backs on what comes with that lineage. To ignore it places us in a position of disobedience and out of order with God. His purpose for us and every being that He created is necessary for the completion of the promises He made. Our faith enables us to believe in that which we cannot see. Hope for the future comes out of believing that life will get better. Our desire and determination drive us to uphold our responsibility to the challenge left to us. We must transform complacency into a thirst for knowledge that moves our children to the next level.

God has equipped us to complete the assignment, but he also has given us free will. We must decide to press forward and to keep our eyes on the prize. We must work while it is still day for night is coming and no work will be done. As a people, we have been lulled into a sense of complacency when we need to be filled with the urgent need for ACTION. Pastor Melvin Dawson, II, founder and senior pastor of Cathedral of Praise, Daytona Beach, recently preached a sermon entitled, "A New Look at an Old Assignment. He pointed out that God has given us all our own personal assignments. Not to be considered by you as a group assignment, i.e., "Someone else can do it if I don't". He also reminded us that a "no" at the wrong time could produce a loss of value for your life. There is always a blessing attached to obedience because there is an anointing attached to your assignment. That anointing demands a "YES". Thirdly, he stated that ALL assignments from God have a "time frame of opportunity". This does not imply that the assignment won't get done but that someone else might get the credit for something that you started. YES, credit does matter. This was a call to action for the church to "work while it is still day", while we still have a chance. There is still time to get your assignment done.

Treyvon Martin, Michael Brown, Eric Garner, Antonio Martin… the list is endless of young black men and women who have been shot and killed by the police and those who think they are the police with no penalties. Not even suspension WITHOUT pay. To suspend someone from work WITH PAY is like sending them on a paid vacation. Where is the punishment in that? We tell our children to follow the rules, to not talk back, to get a good education so they can get a good job, but the reality is that even when they follow the rules, the institutionalization of racism is sometimes an insurmountable wall. They can be killed simply because they are black, ask a question or reach for their driver's license. ON ONE should live in that kind of fear. How do we fix it? How do we overcome 400 years of racist indoctrination that not only is flourishing but causes the victims to blame themselves, hate themselves and lose hope of ever having the opportunities that come with white privilege? Self-hatred is destructive for any people and must be dealt with just like PTS, post traumatic syndrome. The symptoms are the same. We are a people that have been brutalized for generations having no place to hide or just blend in. Society and media promote the evils of blackness and the beauty of "whitedom".

    Black people are told daily that we are too sensitive about racial discrimination, the effects of slavery and that we should "just let it go, get over it". How do you do that? Our story is like no other story on the North American continent. No other people, except maybe the Native Americans, have experienced the separation and decimation of their culture and the connection to their homeland and place of origin. We are not immigrants and did not voluntarily migrate to America and other slave holding countries. We were not given a choice and contrary to what a previous "FLOTUS" might believe, slavery was not "better" than what we came from.

My grandmother understood that if we are to survive the horrors of racism, we must be self-sufficient and self-determining. We must turn the tide on a culture of people "waiting on the mailman" for survival. We are a beautiful and creative people, a chosen people born out of greatness, strength and royalty. Other ethnic groups recognize our strengths and talents and for generations have utilized our skills for their own benefit. We must TEACH our children to own property, to not be afraid to create businesses and step out on FAITH. To plan their work and WORK THEIR PLAN.

The road to generational wealth will not be found at a 9 to 5 job but in multiple streams of income, product development, and control of disposable income. We must stop feeding somebody else's dreams and make our own dreams reality. The accomplishments of Dr. Mary McLeod Bethune were not by chance. They were a fulfilment of her assignment. She did not hesitate to go where she felt God was sending her. She did not question whether or not she could accomplish the goal. She believed that whatever was lacking in her human self, would be more than made up for by the power of God within her. She trusted and never doubted.

With all the proof that God gives us on a daily basis of His existence, we still hesitate. We still question. We still avoid our obligations. Look at your life and think about where you might be if it were not for God's grace and mercy. Think about all the solutions that came just in the nick of time, not because of anything you did, but because of what God connected you to. Think how much better it would be if we just followed His lead and stepped out on His promises.

Too often we are looking at others, coveting what they have and spending too much time wondering "why them and not me". We have taken our eyes off of God and we begin to sink. We have all the tools we need to solve whatever our problems are if we would just use them. Once we connect with our purpose, get busy. If you are a musician, play your instrument. If you are a writer, write. If you are a teacher, teach. No one can do what you do better than you if you focus and believe. Remember, what God has for you, it is for YOU and no one can take it, but you can give it away or miss your opportunity.

In a world that is sometimes filled with a requirement that we all "feel good" and we search for instant gratification, sometimes it is necessary for us to just feel the sadness of life gone too soon, unrealized dreams and lost love. It is ok to just mourn for a time and allow that sadness to connect us to the humanity that has no color, race or creed; no political designations or levels of class; just the connection of our human selves. It is evident that all too often we forget that we are all in this human experience together, finding it all too easy to be disrespectful, hate-filled and on the extreme, murderous.

In the midst of our identity struggles we must always remember to love first. No, it is not easy, but it is necessary. Remembering to love does not mean that we ignore hateful behavior or fall silent in the face of taking a responsible position in the pursuit of freedom and equality for all people. It is because of love that we must stand up for righteousness and truth. We must take a position and not be afraid to defend it, putting God first and always dealing with issues based on Godly principles. Kindness but an expectation of excellence, compassion but insistence on learning to "fish" not just waiting to be given a fish and an attitude of gratitude will help to build a foundation that can support reclamation and revitalization of the human spirit. We MUST teach our children basic principles that will carry them throughout their lives and then insist that they practice what they have been taught.

Love is an action word and it requires that we get up and do something. We must be ready to meet the day to day challenges, equipped with the right words and strengthened by the clear understanding that we are never alone.

Joyce Meyer writes about the importance of how we approach a situation. She says, "Is your problem really your problem or is it your attitude towards your problem that is the problem? Your attitude affects your countenance – your outward appearance."

Strength for the Journey
Dr. Evelyn Bethune

"If we have the courage and tenacity of our forebears, who stood firmly like a rock against the lash of slavery, we shall find a way to do for our day what they did for theirs."
Dr. Mary Mcleod Bethune

"I want to be remembered as someone who used herself and anything she could touch to work for justice and freedom.... I want to be remembered as one who tried." **Dr. Dorothy I. Height**

Change your outlook – Change your life

A POEM FOR MICKEL

Composed by Dr. Evelyn Bethune
With excerpts adapted from –
We Speak Your Names By Pearl Cleage

Mickel ANTONIO Brown, Sr. ...
Because you were a strong man, born of a strong woman. We celebrate your strength
That strong woman, Fannie Williams, also bore another strong woman, your sister, Ericka Dunlap. Ericka will speak your name in recollection of your strength when she feels the need.

Mickel Brown, Sr. ...
We are here because as a husband to Eleanor, your Commitment and dedication to your unconditional love is reflected In the sons you conceived, nurtured, and helped grow into manhood. You sent them out into the world to make their mark and see what you saw, *and be what you be,* but *better, truer, deeper, stronger. Corey, Matthew and Mickel, Jr. are* the shining example of your own incandescent life. We speak your name.

Mickel Brown, Sr. ...
We are here to speak your name because you taught us that the search is always for the truth and that when people show us who they are, we should believe them.
We are here to speak your name because of the path you made for many of us. Because of your willingness to serve, family, friends and strangers.

We are the ones you conjured up, hoping we would have strength enough, and discipline enough, and talent enough, and nerve enough to step into the light when it turned in our direction, and just smile awhile. You reminded us how to laugh with your precious, random thoughts of a THINKING man, filled with humor but pricking our consciousness as well. As a Man thinketh, so is he!

Inspite of your sometimes sadness, you made us dance simply Because we loved the music of times gone by. We will remember dancing under the moonlight at Municipal Stadium as you taught us what real tailgating was all about. We will remember laughing until tears ran down our faces at comedy shows. Who knew that you were the Fred Astaire of Midtown?

Your kindness and your giving spirit will never be forgotten. There are so many people who have been touched by your compassion. We will remember, and we will continue to call your name so that your legacy will continue to live. You entered to learn, departed to serve and now your name has been called from the Book of Life. Mary McLeod Bethune would be proud.
We speak your name...
Mr. Brown, as we fondly called you,

We are the ones you hoped would make you proud, because all of *our* hard work makes all of *your* hard work part of something *better, truer, deeper, stronger.*

You were that Someone willing to carry another until they could carry themselves; that someone that lights the way ahead like a lamp unto our feet, as steady as the unforgettable beat of our collective heart. And those lasting HUGS, HUGS that made you feel that everything was right in the world. Thank you.

We speak your name, Mr. Mickel ANTONIO Brown, Sr. We speak your name. Remembering that as long as we speak your name, you will NEVER, NEVER, NEVER be forgotten. We speak your name.
MICKEL ANTONIO BROWN, SR. *We Speak your name! We speak your name!* **Mr. Mickel ANTONIO Brown, Sr. !!**

On the occasion of the Visitation Memorial Service for
Mr. Mickel Brown Sr.
October 17, 2014
Mary McLeod Bethune Performing Arts Center

You Are Missed – 2018

IN MEMORY OF JARVIS M. SMITH FOUNDER of WAIG JOYGOSPEL 106.3 Rhama Broadcasting Daytona Beach's FIRST 24-hour gospel station

JOY 106.3 FM is Daytona's Favorite Gospel Station. You will experience an awesome blend of worship, contemporary, traditional and today's quartet hits while being informed of community news, upcoming events and the word! WAIG offers competitive sponsorship opportunities for public broadcasting to our local community.

Your support is always welcomed here at WAIG.

For More Information: CALL 386-269-1649

or email us at info@joy1063.com

TUNE IN AND TELL A FRIEND

www.ingramcontent.com/pod-product-compliance
Lightning Source LLC
Chambersburg PA
CBHW051552010526
44118CB00022B/2683